Looking after looked after children

BY JOHN TIMPSON

Published in 2017 by Timpson Limited. 3rd Edition.

Timpson House Claverton Road Wythenshawe Manchester M23 9TT
Tel: 0161 946 6200 www.timpson.com
ISBN: 978-0-9576613-5-6

Written by Sir John Timpson.
Illustrated by Robert Barrow. Printed in Great Britain.

As foster carers and adoptive parents my wife, Alex, and I were always grateful for the help we got from teachers and all the support staff at our children's schools.

John and Alex Timpson

3

The more they knew about the children the less they were surprised by some of their challenging behaviour and the better equipped to help them get the best results.

It is always easier when a classroom is full of well-behaved children.

But that doesn't always happen.

Like many young people, looked after children can have a challenging and confusing way of communicating their thoughts and feelings.

Challenging behaviour can take
several different forms.

LATE

NOT CONCENTRATING

NOT ENGAGED

DISORGANISED

CHALLENGING BEHAVIOUR

There are many more ways children
can use to attract attention.

QUIET EXAM

DISRUPTIVE

SULKING

OVER COMPLIANT

I'm still tidying my desk Miss Smiles.

CLINGY RELIANCE ON ADULTS

As foster carers and adoptive parents we found similar problems at home.

LATE

TEMPER

NOT INVOLVED

SULKY

UNTIDY

STROPPY

It can be tough being a carer.

It can be tough to work in a school.

Unhelpful Citizens

The challenging behaviour of looked after children can be the focus of concern and criticism at school.

NEGATIVE VIBES

Children in care historically have a consistently lower level of academic achievement than other pupils – but performance can improve the longer they are being cared for in a stable home and the more settled they are in school.

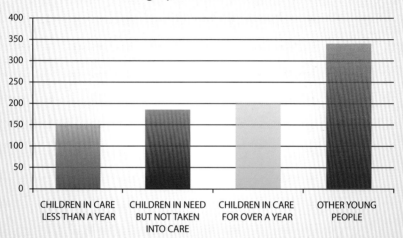

Average points in 8 best GCSE's

Souce: Rees Centre for Research in Fostering and Education

EDUCATION

As carers we sometimes got to the stage
when the task became overwhelming.

Mr & Mrs Helpful

Let us have him for a week, we'll soon sort him out!

Friends can make you feel even worse.

Then we discovered a possible reason for their
challenging and bewildering behaviour.

The day we found out about attachment made a massive difference.

Biology plays an important part but from birth a child's development is shaped by his or her significant relationships.

A baby is totally dependent on adults
for nurture and support.

By constantly satisfying the child's physical and emotional needs an attachment is established and the child feels safe.

Parents usually help their children develop an
emotional attachment - the first two years of
a child's life are very important.

During the early years positive parental attachment forges neural pathways in the brain and provides the basis for social behaviour that will be developed through life.

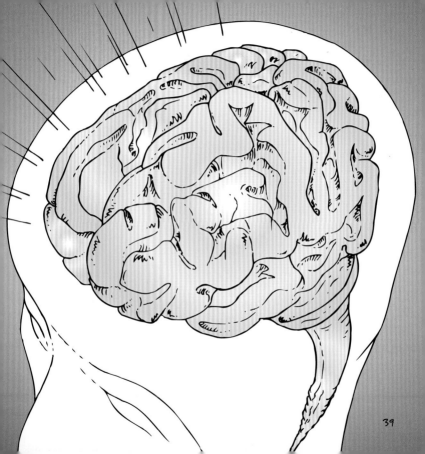

The attachment process continues
when the baby becomes a toddler.

Eventually the child is confident enough to leave the safe base created by the parents and begins to experience independence.

PRE SCHOOL
PLAYGROUP

43

While always knowing there is a warm welcome and safe place waiting at home.

The safe haven continues to be important during teenage years.

With the help of responsive carers children grow up feeling good about themselves and become valued members of society, and are able to form positive relationships.

49

The security of a strong parental attachment helps children trust others and form new relationships with confidence.

51

A strong foundation of emotional confidence helps people become good parents themselves and provide a safe haven for the next generation.

But it doesn't always work like that...

Any child can develop attachment difficulties if there are family problems. Life can be tough and parents aren't always to blame.

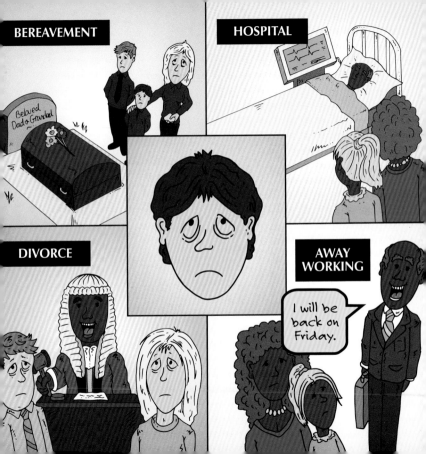

Attachment theory doesn't always explain
a child's challenging behaviour.

AAH

Parents, with a challenging life themselves, find it hard to provide a safe base and help their children to build a positive attachment

DRINK

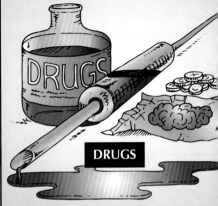

DRUGS

ABSENCE

POOR ROLE MODEL

Shut up and go to sleep!

Instead of getting care and attention the child may be badly treated or ignored. This could cause attachment difficulties.

No cuddles

Physical punishment

Loved one day
Hated the next

Shouted at

Deprived of food

Left alone

No play time

As a result the child feels anxious and unwanted. They think they are unlovable and unworthy of affection. They feel rejected and blame themselves.

The lack of a secure attachment makes the child stressed, unhappy and angry. He could show his feelings through poor behaviour.

The lack of confidence and respect born out of poor attachment in early years can be a burden for years to come.

Many things that are easy for other children can be difficult for those with attachment difficulties.

Scruffy

Smart

LOOKING CLEAN & SMART

!!!???

HOMEWORK BOOK

REVISION

CONCENTRATING

DEALING WITH DIFFICULT SITUATIONS

??**!!/?

The big minibus has broken down so you are one of those that can't go swimming today.

BEING PATIENT

I will be with you when I have finished helping Dawn with her work.

Here are a few more things they
might find pretty tough.

REMEMBERING

BEING ORGANISED

EXPLAINING WHAT THEY MEAN

BEING CONFIDENT

They may find it difficult to get on with other people.

KEEPING COOL

GAINING RESPECT

TRUSTING OTHERS

JOINING IN

They often have a problem finding the right friends.

MAKING FRIENDS

I wonder if Kylie will go out with me?

KEEPING FRIENDS

I don't want to see Kylie anymore!

SOCIAL MEDIA

A lot of your friends are online.

facebook

HANGING OUT WITH THE WRONG CROWD

Don't you realise what they are like?

I don't care, I like them!

Parts of school life can be difficult.

The usual reward and
punishment systems
may not work.

Many find a change in routine disruptive.

NEW CLASSROOM

NEW TEACHER

NEW CLASSMATES

NEW SECONDARY SCHOOL

SCHOOL

83

Great schools don't just stick to statistics, policies and guidelines they have the courage to do what is right to give the pupils the best possible start in life.

MAVERICK HIGHSCHOOL

RATED OUTSTANDING

GREAT SCHOOL

In the same way that wheelchair users need disabled access, some looked after children may need additional support.

VIRTUAL SCHOOL HEAD

I'm here to help looked after pupils build their confidence.

Things at school that can improve the
lives of looked after children.

QUIET ROOM

SAFE SPACE

A place to escape and have some time out.

BUILDING ATTACHMENT

BUILDING ATTACHMENT

CONSISTENCY

Same teacher...

 ...Same place

Same time...

BUILDING ATTACHMENT

One to one relationships.

BUILDING ATTACHMENT

BUILDING ATTACHMENT

Regular link
with carer.

BUILDING ATTACHMENT

Most of all, the pupil needs to form a positive relationship with a member of staff who can become their mentor.

NB. The child should have a big say in choosing their mentor rather than the school picking a staff member with spare time.

So trusted you can form an attachment
and make school a safe place.

There isn't a text book for mentoring - but it
is worth talking to other mentors and their
schools to learn their lessons of success.

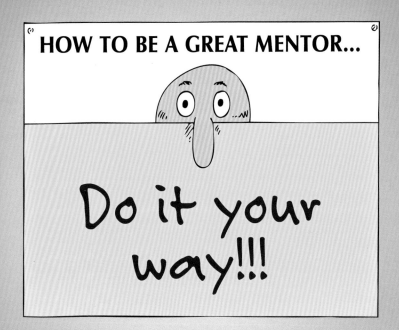

The ultimate manual

A mentor tries to find the key to understand the child and open up the child's positive future.

It's a real privilege to be trusted by the child, to be on their side and help them be the best they can.

Anyone could be chosen as a mentor.

Mentors are ordinary people with
some very special skills.

MENTORS MAKE THEMSELVES AVAILABLE

Can I have a word?

No problem, I've got as long as it takes.

MENTORS LISTEN

It might seem a small thing to you but every time I meet my mates in town I think something is wrong - I am sure they are talking about me behind my back and the next day this girl comes up to me and...

Go on, I'm listening.

Mentors make life fun.

Mentors show they care.

Mentors respect pupils for who they are.

Mentors show they care by wanting to know why.

Mentors must be prepared for the unpredictable.

ME   **THE OTHER ME**

CHARACTERS CAN CHANGE WITH
THE FLICK OF A SWITCH

Mentors don't give up – they are happy to take things a step at a time.

Tell me about it.

Well done!

I was about to blow my top but I took a deep breath and walked away!

A CHAT OVER A SNACK CAN MAKE A DIFFERENCE

They walk beside you.

Mentors are still there when things get tough.

It helps if mentors also have their own mentors to talk to.

MENTOR

MR RELIABLE

A safe base.

The ability to care for and nurture looked after children is a sign of a truly great school.

The individual approach doesn't just work for looked after children – it works for every pupil in the school!!

All staff should feel free to give every
pupil the best education.

Through caring for and nurturing looked after pupils you will put an extra sparkle into the whole school.

120

GOOD LUCK